HR and the Agile Organization

Arlen Bankston

HR and the Agile Organization

Arlen Bankston

ISBN 978-1-387-62784-4

Many thanks to Nate McMahon of the Motley Fool, Tracy Saunders of Ellucian and Jeff Gothelf for your inspiration, stories and time.

Contents

Introduction - A Changing World Needs You

The business world isn't getting, and probably will never get, any simpler or stabler. As a result, agility — the ability to adapt fast — is widely desired. While change is still slow in historically sleepy industries, the majority are struggling to keep up with market disruption and digitization. As much as we'd like to shrug it off, complacency seems an increasingly bad strategy.

Luckily, Agile methods have become a beacon of hope, making change a bit easier. Frameworks like Scrum, Extreme Programming and Kanban arose to maintain a sense of humanity in software delivery, allowing for projects that better matched the natural way that humans work. Agile methods and their precursors are tied to nearly all departments in all industries, from lean manufacturing[1], to medical research[2], quality[3] and management theory, psychology and behavioral engineering[4], human centered design[5] and more.

Agility now reaches far beyond software projects to entire organizations, and the implications span beyond IT teams. Functions like marketing, sales and certainly leadership teams have joined the quest for agility.

So, where does human resources – or the currently ascendant *People Operations* – fit into an agile world? Agile methods are all about people; how to help them collaborate, stay more engaged and focused, work smarter and happier, and adapt with ease and

---

[1] The Machine That Changed the World, Lean Thinking, Womack & Jones
[2] Jeff Sutherland's work as Principal Investigator at the National Cancer Center inspired much of the Scrum framework, which he founded alongside Ken Schwaber.
[3] W. Edwards Deming had a big impact on the early agile founders.
[4] https://appreciativeinquiry.case.edu/intro/whatisai.cfm
[5] http://www.ideou.com/pages/design-thinking

alacrity. These goals align quite readily with what most would consider the goals of modern HR practitioners.

It has even been argued that HR, as classically defined, is in a battle for continued relevancy[6] and survival[7]. Classical functions like recruiting are being automated by software platforms and bolstered by big data, and then there are the younger generations, with a fresh batch of career and life motivations to address. This is less a cause for fear than an evolution and an opportunity.

Human resources professionals have an absolutely critical role to play in hiring, performance management, career development, change management communications and even more if an agile adoption is to succeed. Put simply, HR can build or block agility.

This book will explore how professionals in HR, talent and people operations can build and nurture truly adaptive, happy and agile organizations.

---

[6]https://www2.deloitte.com/content/dam/Deloitte/global/Documents/About-Deloitte/central-europe/ce-global-human-capital-trends.pdf

[7]https://www.fastcompany.com/3045829/the-new-rules-of-work/welcome-to-the-new-era-of-human-resources

Chapter 1 — HR and the Agile Organization

Agile methods took shape in the early 80s, growing from iterative approaches like Rapid Application Development and Spiral Development into methods like Scrum and Extreme Programming. These methods historically focused on improving the performance of teams within development groups, and largely ignored the broader environments in which these teams exist — the "agile organization." This wider purview is where HR comes into play.

Business Agility is a trending term describing what an agile organization might exactly be, used in two basic ways. On one hand, Agile methods are spreading from teams on the IT side to business departments like HR, finance, marketing and sales, with the purpose of making the enterprise a holistically adaptive entity. At its simplest, business agility is defined as non-IT teams using Agile methods. Agile methods can bring a sense order, focus and progress in the face of constant change.

On the other hand, the term business agility is used to describe a holistically adaptive enterprise. Whether or not business-side departments are using agile methods, non-IT units like HR enable broader agility within the organization through quick feedback loops and responsive processes. HR hires and grows the right talent and sets the environment to the culture to thrive. This leads to business agility.

One of the broadest changes that business agility infers is a merging of business and technology functions: a digital transformation. In today's world, technology is a fundamental and proactive tool for learning about the market and using data to drive swift decisions. An agile business is one that has structured itself for the digital age.

There are several ways in which this idea has been expressed, but some consistent patterns emerge:

- Stable cross-functional teams pulling from dynamic backlogs
- Persistent value streams rather than projects delivering core business capabilities
- Managers leading and mentoring people while coaches and teams lead projects

Changing how Teams are Allocated against Work

Building business agility in any department or across the board begins with designing great agile teams. To start, agile teams need cross-functional representation. On an agile IT team, development, analysis and testing capabilities would generally be contained in a single software team. In an HR team, recruitment, professional development and training professionals might work together to deliver a common solution. This protects against waterfall-style serialized handing off of work. End-to-end teams in any department allow for a smoother flow of work, better information sharing, more comprehensive solutions, greater feeling of ownership, quicker adaptation with richer data and more.

Next, teams are built around products rather than projects to give them a longer lifespan. When teams are stable, they can remain gelled and snappily start new endeavors. Work flows to these teams rather than teams moving to the work. Members can of course migrate as teams evolve over time, but new team formation should not be tied to simple project kickoff. When people are not split across many other teams and projects, they can focus. Focus allows for speed.

Third, teams themselves are self-managing, free to shape their path to some extent. Frederic Laloux's book Reinventing Organizations coined the notion of a "Teal" organization, a truly self-managing entity that embodies the principles of self management, wholeness and evolutionary purpose. People who work in such companies, rare though they still may be, tend to be highly engaged and fulfilled. The notion of shaping one's environment, destiny and day-to-day routine rather than being bound by it has clear appeal. Some examples include Morning Star, a large US tomato producer, and Buurtzorg, a Dutch nursing organization. In these firms opportunities for growth are largely limited by the employee's own ambitions.

True teamwork also has a number of psychological benefits. Feeling supported and understood by peers leads to comfort with experimentation and accountability. Blame tends to be greatly diminished when end goals are shared, and fewer hand-offs mean less finger-pointing. Stable, cohered teams are more effective than groups that are still learning how to work together.

These team formation strategies have a direct impact on the HR sphere of influence. Hiring, performance management, resource allocation and incentive design are all areas that require significant attention in an agile organization. Because HR potentially plays a key role in constructing agile teams, it is vital to understand rationale behind agile team construction strategies and the mechanisms by which they are meant to operate.

Aligning around the Value Stream

Rather than form these stable teams around temporary projects, agile organizations align them with product or service lines, called value streams. Value streams describe major capabilities or services against which an efficient structure and flow of delivery can be patterned. They describe the steps in a customer's end to end journey from their initial request to fulfillment (and often beyond).

Value streams are a long standing lean concept embraced by the Scaled Agile Framework[8]. In that method, groups of agile teams deliver via Agile Release Trains which leave on some steady and reliable cadence. These notions are also expressed in the #NoPro-

---

[8]http://www.scaledagileframework.com/value-streams/

jects[9] movement, putting the focus on products over projects. The
value stream is a way not only to amplify delivery, but to learn
rapidly and eliminate wasted time and energy.

The Changing Role of Management

With self-managing agile teams organized around value streams,
who is steering the ship? The focus of management shifts primarily
to people development, moving away from having any real involvement in managing or overseeing daily project work. Their charges
work in persistent agile teams, and leadership positions like the
Scrum Master and Product Owner drive and track project work,
while functional management focuses on personal development and
support activities.

Jeff Sutherland's Scrum at Scale[10] framework encourages managers
to:

- Provide clear and challenging goals for the teams
- Eliminate organizational debt - identify and remove waste
- Create a business plan that works
- Provide all resources the teams need
- Identify and remove impediments for the teams
- Know velocity of teams
- Eliminate technical debt
- Hold Product Owners accountable for value delivered per point
- Hold Scrum Masters accountable for measurable process improvement and team happiness

Managers in an agile organization focus on creating a system
in which improvements are driven by inspiring, supporting and
growing people and their environments. Agile managers avoid

---

[9] https://lithespeed.com/noprojects-need-projects/
[10] https://www.scrumatscale.com/scrum-at-scale-guide/

micromanagement and look to practitioners of the people arts for tools they need to improve systems and grow their people into happy high performers.

Chapter 2 — Qualities of an Agile Organization

I have observed three broad areas where companies are transitioning from traditional qualities to more adaptive, self-organizing, learning behaviors. While not a comprehensive guide, it is meant to echo the Agile Software Development Manifesto — as a *Manifesto for Organizational Agility*.

Dynamic Organizational Design & Leadership

Self-Management over Hierarchy – Localized decision making is faster, more motivating and more scalable when done properly. Keep hierarchies as flat as possible, and support meaningful commitments through clear decision-making policies, dynamic role allocation and pull systems with visible rules.

Wholeness over Work Focus Alone – Support employees' wellbeing, motivation, growth and value orientation by supplying organic, human work environments, hours, workspaces, tools and approaches aligned to a resonating purpose.

Evolutionary Purpose over Static Missions – Agile organizations should be ready to deal with rapidly changing competitive environments and customer needs. Let missions and roles evolve from within by encouraging experimentation and enhancing feedback loops.

Fluid Portfolio Management

Experiments over Business Cases – To save money and improve creative focus, prototype and test ideas before funding them using techniques from the lean startup and Lean UX, or run hackathons. Make this operationally possible through Devops-style integrated, flexible delivery capabilities that span departments.

Product & Service Flow over Transient Projects – To allow for faster starts and more knowledgeable and dynamic working groups, establish stable teams and feed them dynamic flows of work through agile portfolio management processes and enablement of continuous delivery and deployment capabilities.

Informed Product Design

Iteration by Observation over Iteration by Opinion – Get feedback through real-life usage and empirical data, not just internal demos. Adopt continuous delivery, lean startup-style techniques and lean UX.

Holistic Product Teams over Unilateral Product Owners – To drive better innovation and lessen handoffs, use the whole team to drive product design, with facilitative rather than dictatorial leaders, design thinking, collaborative design patterns and story mapping.

While these qualities are vastly different to the way most organizations work today, many of them can be shaped by change agents in HR. Achieving self-management, wholeness and purpose requires the right people, environment, processes, tools and behaviors. I'm sure you're aware, but HR impacts people, environment, processes, tools and behaviors.

Chapter 3 — Thinking with Agility

Note that while HR practitioners do not necessarily have to apply agile methods to their own work in order to support them elsewhere, there are two main reasons to do so. First of all, it is difficult to brilliantly support something you have never experienced yourself. Second, the methods can be as powerful in HR work as they are elsewhere. You might find some of the same benefits that other practitioners enjoy if you employ some of these techniques on your own.

Given the complexity and variety of agile methods, it can be useful to take a step back and simplify the basic concepts. Here are five jargon-free rules to help you grow an agile mindset, along with examples of how they might apply in typical human resources situations.

Understand Value

People who enjoy building (like software teams) are often tempted to feverishly imagine solutions with no thought as to whether they're actually needed. Rampant scope creep evident in projects of every sort has proven time and again that people are pretty poor at making good assumptions upfront. Guessing is easy, and getting good data can be a bother if you don't know how. The rapid feedback loops of agile methods are meant to shore up this problem, but you must know where to look for the feedback. Looking in the right place starts with knowing what value truly means.

Value is multifaceted; common factors include business revenue, cost savings, customer service and stakeholder importance. There is also value in information. Teams learn as they go along — about themselves, their processes and their solution's fit to purpose — and learning tends to accelerate as they gain more experience. All of these components must be balanced to get a clear notion of how to valuate, and therefore how to prioritize.

A simple scenario of this in HR might find you hiring someone for an agile team. A fundamental consideration is what makes that person valuable to the team and the organization. The team wants a person who is highly experienced in agile engineering and coaching in order to mentor a junior associate, which would imply a host of characteristics and job experiences. Boil this down to a few simple factors in order to filter and prioritize, and you have honed in on a definition of value for this particular scenario. You might make this into a fun game-like exercise that you play with the team in question.

Think Big, Build Small

Agile teams build things in small chunks, delivering something tangible every few days or so at most. There are many good reasons to decompose work; small things are easier to discuss, analyze, build, test, document and (critically) change. It is easier to collaborate around something focused and tangible than around something large and ill-defined. Also, teams rally around the feeling of closure and accomplishment that comes from actually getting something done.

Consider building a new performance management system. One tactic might be to spend months planning and crafting in isolation followed by a big, splashy launch. However, this is dangerous and slow; employees may reject the plan, and a revision is a major job, not to mention there is collateral damage.

Tracy Saunders, HR leader at higher education software company Ellucian, developed a successful program in an iterative manner, relying on direct feedback from multiple sets of pilot participants before rolling the program out broadly to a warm reception. She continues to adapt it today.

Focus on Feedback

To move fast, we have to start fast. Many activities get mired before they begin in the muck of analysis paralysis. Nobody knows the answer, but none will admit it. The rationale is fear; if we make a mistake, punishments could ensue so it seems safer to remain perpetually undecided. The solution is to lower the cost of failure and make rapid experimentation safe and palatable. Quick, direct feedback loops are a lovely way to accomplish this.

Feedback is central to the job of developing people. You might lead the development of a self directed learning program that promotes a learning mindset and emphasizes skill development over criticism. Retrospectives could help your team improve in a variety of lively and fulfilling formats.

Work Together

The many activities that comprise building a new product or service are deeply interrelated, and it's tough to manage dependencies with a single hand-off point. Shared roles and activities help team members work fluidly together toward goals they own collectively instead of blaming one another when handoffs go wrong.

Human Resources partners with every department on some level. Map out a few key value streams that involve you, and identify all of the players involved in delivery from idea to final result. Have a workshop with these groups to identify areas where the flow of value is impeded in the form of broken communications, lack of collaboration, unnecessary bureaucracy and so forth. Brainstorm what could be done to improve the situation, then implement formulate some experimental adjustments, tracking and adapting as appropriate. This activity also models the benefits and means of effective cross-departmental collaboration to all involved.

Keep Work Visible

Out of sight, out of mind. When we can't see our work, we forget about it. It lurks in the back of our minds, generating subconscious stresses that drain our energy. Customers get nervous when they can't see the state of their requests, and begin asking for more reports and meetings. The end result is a subtle but draining morass of distrust, lack of focus, wasted time and fatigued despondency. One proven solution is transparency through simple visual management systems that team and stakeholders alike easily find and interpret for themselves.

An HR professional at a Virginia consultancy related his experience using Kanban to manage the hiring and onboarding process:

"The recruiting board we have now is so vastly superior to what we did at my old company. At our company we aren't hiring too many people but at [my previous org] we hired dozens of people a week. We would manually keep spreadsheets and hard copy forms of what we thought of people, where they were in the process and what the next steps were. This was extremely cumbersome and led to a lot of oversights as you can imagine.

Having one board where we could track applicants through the process in job specific swim lanes would have greatly simplified the process and cut down on redundant work. This doesn't necessarily have to be tool specific either. Even if we weren't using LeanKit or another tool, just having a large whiteboard with taped off lanes and sticky notes that all our recruiting team could see would've been superior to our silo (everybody keeping their own records and collating weekly or so) approach."

Kanban for Recruiting

Ready availability of information about work and its status is critical; if we have to hunt to learn something, we often won't bother, especially when it doesn't obviously pertain to us. When information is open for the taking, internal team coordination and external reporting become faster by obviating the need for extraneous meetings and reports.

Chapter 4 — The Role of HR in an Agile Organization

Agile methods are all about people: how to help them collaborate, stay more engaged and focused, work smarter and happier, and make change simple and cheap. These goals align readily with what most would consider those of modern HR practitioners. Unfortunately, HR can also be a huge blocker for agility if not prepared. Outmoded performance management models can pit team members against one another instead of engaging them in a way that encourages collaboration.

The criticality of HR leaders is at an all-time high, a trend reinforced by the increasing prevalence of a CHRO (Chief HR Officer) role reporting directly to the CEO[11]. Contributing to this elevation is the fact that we live in an ever more chaotic world, and businesses need the most capable people they can find and develop to have any hope.

---

[11] https://hbr.org/2015/07/people-before-strategy-a-new-role-for-the-chro

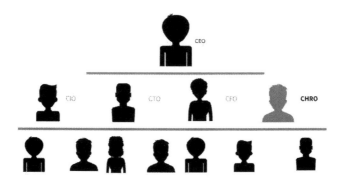

Organizational Leadership

Why Does HR Need to Change?

It has been argued that HR as classically defined is in a battle for continued relevance[12] and survival[13]. Functions like recruiting are being automated by software platforms and bolstered by big data. The younger generations hold a fresh batch of passionately felt career and life motivations to address. This is no cause for fear but an evolution, a challenge and an opportunity to make a more positive and meaningful impact to people's work lives.

There is a movement in the agile space known as *DevOps* which recommends deep alignment between new product development and operations/maintenance activities, departments and leadership. One of the tensions this movement is trying to resolve is that while development groups value speed and change, operations groups historically fight for stability. They should work together.

A tension between finance and human resources has developed due

---

[12] https://www2.deloitte.com/content/dam/Deloitte/global/Documents/About-Deloitte/central-europe/ce-global-human-capital-trends.pdf

[13] https://www.fastcompany.com/3045829/the-new-rules-of-work/welcome-to-the-new-era-of-human-resources

to precisely the same difference in foci. While a CHRO generally looks to drive growth, change and expansion, CFOs are often rooted in more steady-state traditional methods like annualized budgets and scorecards. This tension must be resolved by driving toward common goals, and both roles must work together to drive real change.

If they can free themselves from outmoded administrivia and bureaucracy, HR practitioners can turn their attention to more invigorating and impactful pursuits. Rather than chasing down the latest compliance breach, the focus shifts to strategically improving the business and the lives of those within it.

Visualizing the Case for Change

One way to highlight the need for change to agile methods or anything else is through simple scenario planning. How would your organization react when faced with situations like this?

- A competitor has developed the capability to release products very rapidly, delivering new versions in days versus your company's multi-month average release cycle. What portions of your development lifecycle are keeping you from achieving similar results?
- Demand for top development talent in your area has spiked, making hiring difficult. What does your company offer to young professionals that the competition does not?
- Your company has shifted from delivering a few large, monolithic products to a strategy of creating many small microservices which work together and change frequently. How will our current budgeting and funding process deal with initiatives that take just days or weeks to move from concept to production?
- A dramatic uptick in local traffic has created a need for more flexible work arrangements. How will your company accommodate and align remote and local workers?

- Retention is dropping, and surveys point to a lack of individual engagement and empowerment as the culprit. How does your organization provide for self-directed work and generate a sense of purpose for employees?

These are business problems that have origins and impacts beyond any one department. To solve conundrums like this we need the whole organization to focus on end-to-end agility. You should work with other disciplines to build organizations that are effectively adaptive in the midst of chaos, and intrinsically appealing to those within them.

Agile Organizational Adoption Strategies

Awareness of the patterns for driving an effective agile adoption will help HR practitioners to design change management strategies and determine the proper degree of their personal involvement in the movement.

Involving the Right Players

In the early days of agility, most incursions happened from the bottom up; a team or manager might hear something about Scrum and convince a few others to try it. Assuming all went well things would grow from there. This remains commonplace.

Two problems can arise. Middle management might resist if their roles are unclear. This gap can be spanned through clear communication and a palatable transition plan that emphasizes the benefits of agility, namely a better, more impactful job.

The other problem is lack of executive support. While most executives today at least pay lip service to the purported benefits of agility, they often fail to understand the true scope and import of the change that they're undertaking. Lacking personal experience with agile methods they may not grasp exactly how or why they work, making effective support a much greater challenge and often leading to inadvertent hindrances. They continue to expect detailed end-to-end implementation details of projects before allowing them to get started, where agilists favor a speedy sense and respond approach. Misunderstandings like this lead to many adoptions that stall out, never growing beyond the pilot stage or remaining technology-only initiatives.

You can help by ensuring that there is representation from the top, bottom and middle in any adoption team, and that the full scope of this change is understood by those who will be involved.

Setting and Tracking Goals for Agility

Why should your organization strive to be agile? This is a question that must be asked and answered to provide direction, and to measure agility's positive results against the inevitable cost and pain of changing. Popular goals include greater flexibility, enhanced delivery speed, improved quality, and gaining, retaining and engaging the right talent. Companies place different weights on these priorities, as knowing which is most critical helps highlight whether agility is delivering its ostensible benefits or not. For Capital One's initial agile rollout years ago, CIO Gregor Bailor set an ambitious time-to-market target — 60% or more reduction in delivery time — that made radical change a necessity.

As metrics arrive from teams it is important that they be communicated, good or bad. Positive news help to entice other players and encourage pilot participants with the attention. Bad news surfaces organizational dysfunctions so that they can be alleviated before they really hurt. Impediments to value delivery are highlighted and singled out for improvement, applying agile thinking to the adoption process itself.

HR should have a significant seat at the table of any agile adoption team, with the aims of sprucing up engagement, happiness and learning effectiveness. A sample project might find you enhancing your performance management system, measuring success by engagement ratings from early adopters. Targets tracked on a physical board or big screen would inform iteration of the initiative through frequent review by the adoption team each sprint.

Starting Small vs. Going Big

When rolling out agile methods, the most common approach is to start with a few pilot teams that can be sandboxed and given plenty of support and growing from there. This has the twin advantages of making early successes more likely and allowing for the gradual acquisition and nurturing of agile talent. It can have the disadvantages of becoming a perpetual pilot program if not well shepherded, allowing other silos to continue acting in isolation when agility isn't understood to apply to them. In small companies, switching wholesale can actually be preferable, as it forces everyone to change together.

The right choice is dictated by the complexity of your organization and the level of leadership support that you enjoy for the adoption when getting started. With high support and reasonably low complexity the all-together leap can be preferable, but most organizations still choose the pilot-and-expand model.

A major consideration from an HR perspective is the concern humans hold during a large organizational shift of "what happens to my job?" Adopting agile methods rarely leads to significant downsizing, more often opening up opportunities for new career paths and job possibilities, so that point should be made clear. Illustrating how career progression will change is critical, so individuals can begin making plans for how they might like to participate. Agility holds many potential benefits for employees, such a more natural approach to work and more freedom in many respects, but touting these jewels is only helpful so long as people believe there will be a place for them in this shiny new world.

Summary - HR for the Agile Organization

You can't stop change, but you can make it more agreeable. Agile methods such as Scrum brought homo sapiens back into the process of software development, taught them that failure was a learning opportunity, and gave them tools to master the art of living with fluidity.

After years of evolution and adaptation these methods are now being adopted far and wide: across business functions, throughout industries and even within personal lives. One core reason for this universal appeal is that they are more a way of thinking than simply a process toolkit. The holistic, cross-departmental impact of a new strategic mindset means that HR involvement is critical in any organization that is considering adopting agile methods.

Agile organizations aim to be aligned more toward customer needs, with silo-free structures that align dependent functions into value streams. Management supports small, stable cross-functional teams by creating an environment where they can more easily collaborate.

HR professionals should understand and be equipped to support agile initiatives because of their widespread impact. Large adoptions can imply substantial and rapid change requiring training, mentoring and communication. Hiring and nurturing talent in a continuous manner is key to successful agility.

Activities to Try

Illustrate a Value Stream Map for the Big Picture

Value streams describe the complete flow of activities that plan, create and deliver the core products and services of your organization. Creating one that describes the streams your HR group crosses is a great way to start getting a handle on the scope of impact you can expect from an expansion of agile methods. Note that this activity will work best if facilitated by someone familiar with value stream mapping.

1. Detail the services and product categories that you offer most (e.g. recruiting, learning management systems), starting from a customer's perspective and then detailing out support functions.
2. Construct a small team (preferably less than 10 people) containing the core skills needed to deliver capabilities within one of these value streams. Note that this will certainly involve other departments; highlighting dependencies between groups is a key part of the activity.
3. Note the key goals of the value stream; how would you most directly measure success?
4. Have representatives from each department sketch out their processes.
5. "Go to the Gemba" (a lean term for shop floor) to validate the accuracy of the map. This means either participating in or watching the process in action to ensure that the description isn't missing key details. It almost certainly will be at first.
6. Note how long each step takes, and the calendar time that elapses between each step. This is often related to places where queues form, perhaps for approval or when hand-offs occur between groups.
7. Illustrate places where flow seems to be impeded.
8. Pick a few of these places, and brainstorm some ways in which you can clear the path for value to flow more smoothly. This might imply more cross-functional teams, joint planning sessions, realignments of ownership and more.
9. Get started improving, and don't forget to iterate and adapt!

Visualize your Strategy with an Impact Map

Impact maps are simple charts that align a plan with the needs of the actors that it affects and your organizational goals. They are quick and easy to create, just a few hours of effort.

1. Gather stakeholders involved in your next job.

2. Define the Goal, or core value proposition of your effort.

3. List and prioritize potential Actors: the primary customers, users and beneficiary stakeholders of your effort.

4. List as Impacts the ways in which you will change each actor's behaviors or outcomes. These should be measurable and quantifiable, such as reducing the time it takes to do a task, or improving satisfaction ratings. Prioritize these as well.

5. Brainstorm deliverables that might help deliver the desired Impacts. You know the drill by now; prioritize them, and now you have the start of a Product Backlog!

Write a Story Map for Change

Craft a compelling tale about how business agility affects the HR function and organization and how it impacts HR team members' roles and behaviors. This can help to guide your participation in any change management activities related to your agile adoption.

1. Gather information about users' problems, motivations and current activities (the Impact Map above would be an excellent starting point).

2. Map out high-level jobs or activities you might create or improve for them using sticky notes in simple rows on the wall.

3. Brainstorm detailed solutions with your team, and cluster these into tight, logical groupings underneath the jobs.

4. Plan the simplest experience that meets the goal for an initial release, with the intent to flesh it out in subsequent releases based upon feedback.

Focus (and kill a boring meeting) with a Story Board

You know that weekly status meeting that you hold? Perhaps it could be a bit more action-oriented and deal less with issues of status if you were to implement a few simple information radiators, such as:

- Story or Task Board - What are we working on? What's most important?
- Burndown or Burnup charts - How are we progressing against our goals?
- Blockers - What problems do we have, and what are we doing about them?
- Working Agreements - How do we like to work together?

Try building a simple User Story Tracking board with your team as follows:

1. Write down current jobs, their customers and value propositions in a few words, describing one job per sticky. Limit to about two jobs per person in your team at first to keep focus. We'll call these Stories.
2. On a wall or whiteboard, draw columns and label them with the key states through which jobs travel (e.g. not started, doing, reviewing, done). Put the Stories in the appropriate columns.
3. Have a quick daily stand-up meeting at that location with your team.
4. Note key questions that stakeholders will likely ask about the project (e.g. when will it be done? What's happening now?), and discuss those with your team.
5. Draw a simple chart of the team's delivery trends to date, with stories finished on one axis and time on the other.
6. Project forecasts of the near future with these trends with a simple range, such as our HR team finishes 5-6 stories on average per two-week sprint. Share this with stakeholders to keep them apprised of progress.

Transparency is determined by the relevance, understandability and availability of information about work being performed. Information radiators such as Story Boards and are meant to be automatic status conveyors for both teams and their customers.

Test Assumptions with a Customer Intercept

Many projects fail simply because the assumptions that they've made turn out to be untrue. Teach your teams how to build and run quick experiments to avoid this problem. This entire process can be done well in just a few days with some experience.

1. Pick one of your current jobs and convene a few members of your team that are good at interviewing and understanding people.
2. Brainstorm assumptions you're making about your audience, the nature of their problems or the solution being considered.
3. Write these down as hypotheses, and rank them by risk.
4. Run a collaborative design session, having each team member draw out a potential experiment to test these assumptions, silently and within a timebox.
5. Have them share their ideas, then run another round and encourage people to steal ideas freely from others. Run one final round, and you should have some great experiments to run.
6. Create simple sketches, prototypes, simulations and research plans as appropriate to prepare for your experiment. Keep the plans quick and viable; we want results in days, not weeks or months.
7. Update your business case, backlog of solutions, priorities and stakeholder expectations as appropriate based on this new knowledge of what is truly most valuable, and to whom.

Chapter 5 — Hiring for Agility

What makes someone ideal for the agile organization? The word *agile* means flexible, pointing to one essential quality you'd hope to see; someone who can work well in the midst of rapid, sometimes disruptive change. Learn how to identify and attract people who will thrive in an agile environment, and come up with clever ways to welcome them when they arrive.

Who handles hiring and firing in general in an agile organization? In general the answer here remains *whomever did it previously,* usually functional managers. In more progressive organizations teams might also make these decisions more directly. Leadership roles like the Scrum Master and Product Owner influence these activities to some degree but rarely control them, largely to retain a sense of trust and safety with their teams.

Here are some guidelines for creating an agile-friendly recruiting and onboarding pipeline.

Recruiting

It is steadily more difficult for staid, bureaucratic companies to attract the best talent. As it so happens, companies that advertise an agile way of working tend to do quite well in this respect, all else being equal. As your prospects multiply there are certain qualities you'll want to see that will make them more or less suited to an agile environment.

Qualities of Great Agile Team Members

Agile teams are purposeful melting pots that join different skill sets, perspectives and activities in a complementary way. People work together via techniques like pairing, swarming[14] and mob programming[15]. They're good at completing a few things at once in a focused manner, rather than starting lots while finishing little. They take measured chances with courage, understanding that improvement and innovation require occasional failures.

Ideal denizens of an agile team share some common traits:

- Comfort with diverse viewpoints
- Flexibility in approach
- Love for learning
- Ability to collaborate
- Self discipline
- Willingness to adapt to regular feedback on one's product, process and person

Prospects need not be adept at all of these facets, but if substantially weak in many they are unlikely to work well in an agile environment.

Qualities of a Great Scrum Master or Agile Coach

The Scrum Master is a coaching and facilitation role whose main function is not direction and control, but enablement of self-management in others. Jeff Sutherland describes the job simply:

- Remove impediments
- Guide the team in Scrum practices
- Protect against outside interference

---

[14] https://www.infoq.com/news/2013/02/swarming-agile-teams-deliver
[15] ttp://mobprogramming.org

What makes someone good at these tasks? Scrum Masters are often cast as "servant leaders." This concept is echoed in Les McKeown's idea of "The Synergist"[16] leadership style:

"The Synergist brings a primary focus on what is best for the enterprise as a whole, and they choreograph and harmonize team or group interactions to produce high-quality decisions. Adding the Synergist style to a VOP (Visionary–Operator–Processor) group releases it from the gravitational pull of gridlock and compromise, and transforms it into a high-performance team."

Agile thought leader Mike Cohn relates the Scrum Master to a personal trainer[17] or bandleader[18]. As a process coach, the Scrum Master makes sure that proper form and techniques are being utilized to keep things safe, ensures people meet the commitments they've made for themselves, and provides expert guidance. The Scrum Master cannot force the team to do things, only control the environment and encourage the right way through convincing argument and demonstration.

Band leaders synchronize disparate parts into an effective whole. They create a dynamic supportive structure where everyone can contribute according to their capabilities while focusing on the quality of the performance above all. Scrum Masters create safe environments where teams can explore new ways of working with confidence, taking calculated risks to adapt and improve without gambling their careers. Simon Sinek makes the point[19] that a pivotal quality of good leaders is the ability to create a feeling of safety.

---

[16] www.predictablesuccess.com

[17] https://www.mountaingoatsoftware.com/agile/scrum/scrummaster

[18] http://www.mountaingoatsoftware.com/articles/leader-of-the-band

[19] https://www.ted.com/talks/simon_sinek_why_good_leaders_make_you_feel_safe/transcript?language=en

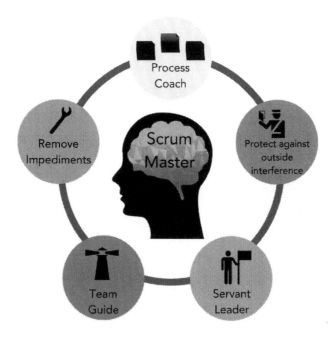

A Great Scrum Master

A great Scrum Master (whether Synergist, coach, personal trainer, army captain or bandleader) is:

- Comfortable with groups and constructively collaborative
- Emotionally intelligent, humble and good at developing and managing relationships
- Strong at reading and guiding both individual and group dynamics
- Silently persuasive and confident with both team members and stakeholders
- Focused on making others succeed rather than oneself, humble
- Driven by the pursuit of continuous improvement

- Effectively analytical in a targeted and flexible manner, able to visualize improvement opportunities through both subjective and objective information
- A great bidirectional communicator, a builder of potent feedback loops
- Transparent and honest, implicitly trustworthy
- Focused on empowerment and self-management over control and direction
- Technically and intellectually facile with the tools of the trade; sources of advice must demonstrate competence and knowledgeability
- Responsible, as to hold others accountable one should lead by example

Scrum Masters should be leaders of people, masters of systems, boosters of learning, builders of teams, and mentors of apprentices. A heady job when done well!

Qualities of a Great Product Owner

The Product Owner (PO) is a role meant to mindfully manage the limited supply of the team to the fundamentally infinite demand of market and stakeholders. As with any agile role, we'd prefer to see ambassadors than dictators, and compelling arguments beat implacable demands.

Product Owners promote a vision of what a product or service might be, while correcting to what it should be through feedback from users, customers, team and market. Teams help to explore the problem space through prototyping, information gathering and collaborative refinement of backlog items. So, while the PO role often sounds like a solo affair, it is in fact deeply collaborative when done well.

A role analogous to the perfect PO can be found in Toyota's Chief Engineer, a senior leader deeply experienced in both engineering and organizational management that guides the development of a new car. John Shook of the Lean Enterprise Institute spoke to the egalitarian nature of the role and the soft leadership skills[20] it requires:

"He is unable to simply pull rank, to put his foot down and demand that the functions do as he demands. Functional resources can and do tell him 'no' if and when they have a good reason. He can only lead by being knowledgeable, proposing good ideas, expertly negotiating multiple priorities and wishes, and being very strong. In short, he has to lead by exercising true leadership skills, not relying on the authority vested in him by virtue of his position on an organizational chart."

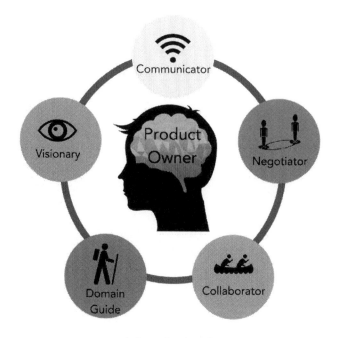

A Great Product Owner

---

[20]http://www.lean.org/shook/DisplayObject.cfm?o=906

Personal characteristics one might like to see in a Product Owner include:

- Compelling visionary, able to set ambitious goals that inspire a team beyond simple construction to mental and emotional engagement
- Powerful communicator and negotiator who can make the case for changing priorities, removing features, releasing early and other potentially controversial moves
- Politically astute, able to navigate shoals of stakeholders and sandbars of conflict while making strong decisions that stick
- Able to understand the domain; note that this does not necessarily require deep expertise upfront, but rather the ability to understand a problem space sufficiently to guide iterative exploration and gain access to the right experts
- Focused and biased towards action, so that deliveries and their resultant feedback loops are frequent and reliable
- Sufficiently humble to change direction and take guidance based on convincing information from the team or customers
- Strongly responsible and prepared, as this position often becomes a bottleneck when done without proper energy, foresight and rapidity
- Able to work collaboratively with a team to bring out their best, rather than trying to be an army of one or a unilateral commander

The Product Owner is similar in many ways to the Scrum Master, a coach of product in this case that guides a team towards the light in the face of discovery and redirection.

Qualities of a Great Agile Leader

Agile leadership is among the most critical yet poorly addressed roles of all. Without understanding and support from the top teams can become disempowered, disconnected from one another and the market, mired in organizational dysfunction, and ultimately despondent and limited in what they can achieve.

An agile leader must build and nurture systems in which teams can maximize their potential, providing audacious strategic goals while clearing the way for teams to effectively self-manage. Scrum Masters and Product Owners are team leaders; organizational leaders require similar skills exercised at a higher level.

Inspired by the clarity of the Agile Manifesto[21], a group of luminaries including Agile Leadership Academy®[22] cofounder Sanjiv Augustine wrote the Declaration of Interdependence[23] to illustrate the duties of a project manager or leader in an agile environment:

- Increase return on investment by making continuous flow of value our focus.
- Deliver reliable results by engaging customers in frequent interactions and shared ownership.
- Expect uncertainty and manage for it through iterations, anticipation and adaptation.
- Unleash creativity and innovation by recognizing that individuals are the ultimate source of value, and creating an environment where they can make a difference.
- Boost performance through group accountability for results and shared responsibility for team effectiveness.
- Improve effectiveness and reliability through situationally specific strategies, processes and practices.

Considering the executive level specifically, the Agile Leadership Academy notes that an Agile Leader must manage the following jobs:

---

[21] http://agilemanifesto.org
[22] http://www.agileleadershipacademy.com
[23] http://pmdoi.org

- *People Operations* – Supplying an agile environment and personal opportunities. This could include open workspaces, flexible working hours, open vacation policies, — and clear delineation of career paths.
- *Self-Management* – Managing systems and coaching people. Creating autonomous yet aligned teams, self-reporting visual management systems, lean standard work processes and more are all examples of this skill.
- *Personal Presence* – Leading with purpose. Daniel Goleman describes in his book *Focus*[24] the qualities of inner, outer and other focus; balancing various perspectives to understand one's people, environment and self.

---

[24] https://www.amazon.com/Focus-Hidden-Excellence-Daniel-Goleman-ebook/dp/B00BATG220

A Great Agile Leader

These responsibilities imply a number of personal traits that would constitute a desirable Agile Leader:

- Learn continuously and adapt to changing situations and needs with creative solutions
- Focus on developing people over enforcing processes
- Communicate clearly about desired goals and the rationale for their priority, without over-specifying how they can be achieved
- Understand and engage with a diverse spectrum of stakeholders effectively to create flow and enhance collaboration across teams and silos
- Base critical decisions more on objective data than on subjective opinions

An agile leader must build flexible but resilient systems in which teams can act independently with confidence, and within which individuals can exercise their creativity and grow to their maximum potential. Disconnected order issuers need not apply; this role requires vision and strategic knowledge, but also empathy and trust.

Agile Onboarding

The fleetness of agile organizations means getting new hires ready to roll as quickly as possible. Of course we'd like to make it fun, involving and memorable while we're at it. To this end, many companies have invented boot camps and game-like training simulations to help immerse and orient new hires directly and without long-term overhead.

While there is no official agile approach to onboarding, organizations often favor rapid immersion to introduce people and culture, incorporating direct practice with the basic tools and skills needed to effectively begin work. Provision of robust self-led learning and self-setup capabilities has also become very popular.

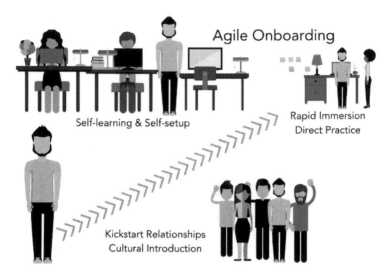

Agile Onboarding

At The Motley Fool, new employees start on a Friday, handling the basic paperwork first thing in the morning to get the drudgery out the way. Then they head out with a *Beverage Cart* to meet and feed everyone. This informal but personal touchpoint is a fast and fun way to establish a feeling of familiarity and kickstart relationships. At the end of day, the new Fools go home with a $100 dinner gift certificate as one more reason for significant others to feel good about the fresh start too.

Starting with a team on Monday, the newbie get paired with a Fool that leads a puzzle-strewn scavenger hunt designed by the Chief Collaboration Officer. This helps them learn about the company as they list the products the company offers for the next clue. Playing is faster and more engaging than sitting through a multi-hour Powerpoint presentation, especially working alongside both equally clueless fellow freshmen and adroit alumni. New employees are asked whom they admire, and this has led to on-site talks by Adam Grant, Dan Pink, Roy Spence, and Elon Musk, to name a few.

GitHub does *lightning profiles* of new hires to whip out the welcoming mat and get folks talking. Peter Furia[25] notes "the first step of communication is an introduction; we've all been at parties where people mill about each other awkwardly, not feeling open to conversation because they weren't introduced." They do bite-sized training videos to make learning basic tools and techniques self-serve, and profiles of inspiring women in the field called Passion Projects.

The thread running through all of these stories is immersion and excitement. New employees find themselves in a safe environment where they can directly experience how the company operates in a threat free manner.

Summary - Hiring for Agility

The most successful participants in agile organizations are disciplined communicators, collaborators and learners. A great Scrum Master is a servant leader that helps others perform better and is good at driving improvement efforts. A great Product Owner is a visionary leader who is excellent at stakeholder and product management. A great Agile Leader understands systems thinking and can create an environment where self-management and growth is strongly supported. Given this environment, the one remaining factor to consider is how to most effectively work together.

Activities to Try

Design an Onboarding Game

This is a fun one, and can yield both interesting new tricks to try while hiring and a collaborative design experience for your team that is often employed in agile circles.

---

[25] https://www.fastcompany.com/3020181/open-company/inside-githubs-super-lean-management-strategy-and-how-it-drives-innovation

1. Gather your HR team for a half-day workshop.
2. Illustrate the current onboarding process together, using stickies on a wall.
3. As a team, brainstorm pros and cons of the current onboarding process, writing them on stickies and placing them above or below the relevant steps in the process.
4. Individually, silently and within a 30 minute timebox, team members sketch out at least two interactive games or exercises for onboarding that might address inadequacies noted in the current system.
5. Show and tell the ideas together.
6. Run another round of silent sketching, and have team members either adapt their existing games or create new ones based upon what they learned.
7. Have team members vote on the candidates at this point, and pick the top three.
8. Separate into three teams, and flesh these candidates out into more complete games.

If you really want to enhance this exercise, have team members read the book "Design Your Own Games and Activities" by Dr. Sivasailam "Thiagi" Thiagarajan prior to the session. It's 400 pages, but worth it, so give them plenty of time beforehand!

Hunt the Agile Wumpus

Hunt the Wumpus was an early text-based computer game where you had just two possible actions to move through an invisible maze and avoid a monster: shoot and move. The results of your actions would fill in the picture of the maze and its obstacles, and you could use logic to succeed. This process amounts to the experimental, data-based approach espoused in most agile methods.

This exercise will challenge your team to find a few great agilists by creating a clever hunting plan.

1. Present your team with the qualities of great agile team members, coaches, product owners, and leaders noted above.
2. Have them brainstorm the places in which these beasts might dwell and their habits. Bonus points for pictures here.
3. Have team members individually concoct strategies for locating, enticing and filtering these potential candidates, then place them in a gallery on the wall.
4. Have a brief gallery exhibition where team members explain their ideas, one minute per idea.
5. Give ten minutes for the team to write comments on stickies about details they like within each idea.
6. Form two teams and have them create two different ideas based upon any or all of the design candidates, modified as they see fit.
7. Try both of these ideas and review the results within a month or two.

Activities like this can encourage a more holistic perspective on hiring, and they also encourage ongoing creativity.

Create Agile Hiring Personas

One popular technique utilized in agile projects is the creation of "personas" to represent various actors. These give a name, face and backstory to potential customers for whom you're building a solution. In this exercise your team will use them to visualize ideal targets for hiring and recruiting.

1. Create a one-page template with the following information:
   a. Name, Age, Gender, Location, Job Title
   b. Job description
   c. Goals of your job (top three)
   d. Concerns and Pain Points (top three)
   e. A quote detailing their core objectives
   f. Feature/Capability Requests (top three)

2. Break your team into three groups, and give each one of the templates. One group will focus on ScrumMasters/Coaches, another will focus on Product Owners, and the third will focus on Agile Leaders.
3. Fill in these templates separately in each group for 15 minutes.
4. Rotate the groups and have them comment on one another's templates for 5 minutes.
5. Rotate once more, so that every group has commented on every persona.
6. Place the personas somewhere public (e.g. posters on the wall), and use them as tools to guide hiring. Adapt them as appropriate as you learn.

This is a quick, entertaining way to orient a team around their end customers' needs, thus avoiding the common problem of diving straight into solution design.

Chapter 6 — Working Together Effectively

Creating a Collaborative Environment

An agile environment facilitates easy collaboration within and across groups while still providing private spaces, and provides the proper tools and guidance to support a distributed workforce even when most are local.

The Case for Collocation

Agile methods such as Extreme Programming and Scrum emphasize the joys of co-locating team members in a common space. They increase the opportunity, bandwidth and quality of interactions when done well. While this still rings true today, improvements in collaboration technology alongside accommodating attitudes and aptitude have made remote work a generously more viable scenario than it used to be.

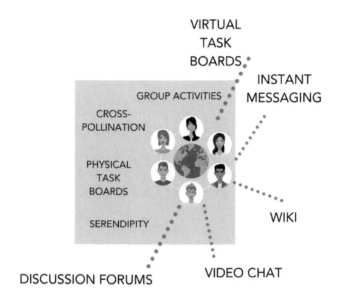

Remote vs Collocated Communication

There are elements of collocation that remain difficult to replicate in a purely remote working environment, namely:

- *Serendipity* - Randomly overhearing something that emerges as potentially useful to you is an event that happens more often than you might think within high-functioning agile teams.
- *Cross-pollination* - Having people with different roles work alongside one another tends to lead to skill sharing by chance and availability. When assistance is expected, it is more readily requested.
- *Interactive group activities* - Events like early discovery work and team-building, release planning and anything social are tough to equal virtually, a key reason why even heavily

distributed environments try to bring people together for such things.

- *Effective information radiation* - While there are plenty of digital agile tools out there and some are great, people can still be hesitant to try something new, especially when it seems to up their workload. But if a few words per day in a quick meeting (daily scrum) is all that's needed to keep the board current it seems less of a chore. People don't tend to open tools just to check status, so they often get minimal use, while readily accessible physical boards are more frequently utilized.

The simplest advice here is to collocate for events that require a great deal of complex interaction, such as planning and launching new initiatives, and occasionally for purposes of team building. However, especially in high-traffic urban environments, giving people the flexibility to work from wherever they are has undeniable benefits. As with anything, experiment and find the proper balance for your organization.

Facilitating Distributed Collaboration

Having team members located physically distant from one another is less of a challenge than it once was, but there are still issues to be addressed.

Some level of basic human familiarity among team members tends to be very helpful when people are expected to trust one another and readily collaborate. Many teams that end up scattered around the world still try to get together physically when the project is first being launched. This lets members make a personal connection, surface behavioral idiosyncrasies when easily recognized and addressed, and tune the way they work together in an intense kickoff that will help set them up for their eventual dispersion.

The day to day work of an agile team can be accomplished nicely in a remote setting. Even when team members are sitting next to one another, it's commonplace for channels like Slack and messaging apps to carry plenty of chatter. A communication and knowledge management setup might look something like this:

- A wiki like Atlassian's Confluence for capturing persistent, unstructured information
- A discussion forum like Slack for ongoing, multi-party conversations
- An instant messaging tool like HipChat for real-time communication among team members
- Minimal usage of email except for simple reminders

When complex or strategic matters must be discussed it is better done in a live format of some sort. If not face to face, then in some bidirectional forum like Google Hangouts. The more asynchronous the discussion (email) the longer it will take, and the less likely that it will lead to coherent, elegant outcomes. For convoluted, controversial or nebulous exchanges shoot for the highest bandwidth communication possible.

Agile Performance Management Systems

Traditional performance management systems focus heavily on the individual. Consider the bigger picture. We don't simply want multiple perspectives on a person, we want to measure outcomes at the team, customer and organizational levels. Behaviors like supporting teammates in unexpected ways and proactively crossing silos should be rewarded, rather than subordinated to fixed personal or managerial goals.

An agile organization needs a growth mindset, and performance management processes should reflect this thinking. Fixed mindsets hold that people are born great (or not) and rely on innate abilities, while growth mindsets purport that talent can and should be nurtured through intentional effort. Fixed mindsets tend to lead to defensiveness and personal retrenching in the face of feedback while growth-oriented people more readily accept whatever is needed to improve as opportunities rather than threats. We should ensure that feedback mechanisms pursue efforts and not just results.

An agile performance management system should:

- Separate feedback mechanisms from basic compensation and legal cover
- Involve knowledge workers in determining their own measurement criteria
- Consider holistic perspectives from team members, customers, users and managers
- Accommodate changing jobs, differing levels of performance & situational leadership
- Collect feedback frequently and use it to improve product & process continuously

Designing Effective Feedback Systems

Feedback should be fast, easy and visibly acted upon on a regular basis. Formal evaluations are typically demotivating by focusing on weaknesses rather than strengths. Annual reviews fail the speed criterion and end up irrelevant to real improvement. In agile organizations feedback loops require less ceremony while focusing on making the interaction demonstrably valuable for both reviewer and recipient.

Fundamental to agility is self management, and timely, quality information is needed to make the right decisions and grow personally while aligning well with team and organization.

A former HR manager turned operations guru reflected and compared:

"Like most companies we had the typical performance management model where you would write you goals at the beginning of the fiscal year and perhaps once or twice during the year you would meet with your manager to see if you were on track to meet those goals. The whole process really turns into a sham where no meaningful, specific feedback could be given because you're meeting so infrequently and people forget.

Changing the system to a continuous feedback stream would certainly take a lot of buy in from upper management, but it's vastly superior. If we could've had a quarterly survey where we rate our peers in certain categories and had mechanisms for following those ratings up with meaningful conversations about self and corporate improvement, rather than something that was a formality (yearly reviews), we could've turned it into an engine for rapid improvement and introspection."

Feedback systems need feedback themselves. Google's People Operations famously relies on data about what really works to drive their approach, which allows them to truly fine tune their tactics to the needs of the present. Think of data you might gather and use in a similar fashion.

Intrinsic Motivators Drive Engagement

When employees can't request help and get it quickly they either stop improving or start leaving. The large cost of hiring new people relative to that of keeping the good ones makes the importance of this situation obvious. Designing a feedback system that focuses on intrinsic motivations while trying to clear away demotivators can bolster retention and engagement. In his book "Drive,"[26] Dan Pink suggests that the three major factors of motivation are autonomy, mastery and purpose; control over your destiny, room to grow and

---

[26] http://www.danpink.com/books/drive/

a North Star to guide you.

What we would like to do is get people to largely manage them-selves, reaching out when they need help instead of hiding and hoping not to fail. This means getting them engaged and excited about their work, looking for opportunities where they can improve both themselves and their contexts on an active and ongoing basis. Those who choose their own plans are more likely to see them through and learn from their stumbles en route.

Development Conversations

Where can we introduce or provide employees with new paths forward that will rekindle their love for their work and let them make a real difference? Here are some questions to highlight intrinsic motivators:

- What are you passionate about doing? (Provides purpose, guides mastery)
- What degree of control do you have over when and with whom do you work? (Autonomy, camaraderie)
- How much control do you have creatively in your work? (Purpose, autonomy, mastery)

It is also useful to examine how current activities are aligning with personal and organizational goals. Author and professor Dan Ariely in an entertaining TED video called "What Makes Us Feel Good About Our Work"[27] notes that simply reviewing people's work is motivating, even in the absence of terribly meaningful feedback. While that's not too surprising, he also found that a complete lack of review - ignoring people's work altogether - was a huge demotivator, nearly equivalent to literally shredding their work before their eyes upon completion.

To avoid this sad result, you might ask:

---

[27] https://www.ted.com/talks/dan_ariely_what_makes_us_feel_good_about_our_work

- What has been achieved and learned since last we met?
- How have clients and market responded to your efforts and those of your team?

With information such as this in hand a conversation can be had about a few things to stop, start, continue, amplify or diminish before you both meet again next month. These adjustments become Stories which will become the basis for career and personal development.

Inspired by Laszlo Bock's book *Work Rules*,[28] the Motley Fool aims for employee development over assessment. Guided by principles of growth mindset, compassion and an employee-driven focus, managers and their direct reports hold regular personal development conversations. Based on a holistic blend of self-assessment, manager and peer assessment, employees are placed in one of the following Development Conversation Zones:

- *Discover* - What are some things people can do beyond their current job responsibilities? Do they have hidden skills which might be usefully employed?
- *Challenge* - Someone who is trying to explore new areas might need some guidance to achieve full mastery.
- *Unleash* - Where people have a strong grasp of their work, find what they want to do and clear the way for them to do it.
- *Shift* - Where employees are employing effort without results, they may be in the wrong role. Find them somewhere where their unrealized potential can be unleashed.
- *Worry* - Someone is neither trying very hard nor succeeding. They need a tough but compassionate conversation and guidance on an urgent plan to correct.

---

[28] www.workrules.net

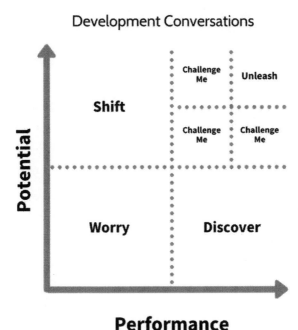

Development Conversations

Performance

Development Conversation Zones

These are a powerful tool to align managers and their direct reports, because they ensure that both people agree on the nature of the existing situation ("Zone") before starting the conversation on next steps. the Fool has deployed a survey asking whether employees get "clear messages about how they're performing," and so far the results are encouraging.

HR leader Tracy Saunders describes a similar agile-inspired feedback system at Ellucian:

"Using an agile approach, during our 'A meetings' we take a look back at the past 90-days and look forward 90-days to make sure our team members have clear expectations and are focusing on what

matters most. We integrated the latest findings from neuroscience to create the psychological safety which allows for more peer-like discussions. The conversation is expanded to not only focus on goal attainment, including development goals, but to also align on behaviors that are consistent with our values. This is also an opportunity to discuss career aspirations."

These systems have the common qualities of frequency, an eye toward personal growth in unforeseen directions, clear direction on alignment with company needs, and a compassionate style.

Peer Feedback Structures and Patterns

It is important to work together, and easy, effective peer feedback informs and tunes this process. At one Virginia consultancy a simple "recognitions" system is employed wherein employees give one another "pennies" for anything they feel is noteworthy via tiny emails. These are appreciations for assistance, admiration of exceptional performance, laudings of leadership and notes of uplifting attitudes. Each quarter, the pennies are tallied and have a tiny impact on the profit sharing system. However, at the team's own behest it is mostly a symbolic action that helps everyone realize what is most valued by their peers.

In addition to micro feedback, mentoring programs are commonplace. Mentors tend to rotate as employees desire new roles and skills. Ensure that regular access to feedback from both a managerial and peer perspective is available and that support is provided for implementing any proposed adjustments.

Compensation, Rewards and Incentives

In order to drive collaboration one should visibly value it. This means that reward and recognition systems must consider the performance of people within and for their teams, and avoid placing employees in a position where working together works to their detriment. Typical management by objective schemes usually fall afoul of this by assigning incentives based upon overly narrow and fixed individual targets.

Some of the best rewards aren't monetary, but based in freedom and recognition. Some examples might be the chance to choose your next project, an email to everyone about a stellar contribution, or a surprise batch of cupcakes. Look once more to autonomy, mastery and purpose, as these are opportunities to enhance a person's natural motivation, and then simply show people that you and their peers are paying attention.

On the flipside, Trevor Owens argues in The Lean Enterprise[29] that truly entrepreneurial types are driven by money and achievement. A glance at the media image of Silicon Valley provides some clear support for his perspective. His "innovation colonies" are enriched directly from their work or feel its failure like independent companies.

Another compelling freedom is choosing your own place and time to work. Given the travails of modern commutes in metropolitan areas even a day or two working from home can be a major motivator and improve productivity by allowing people to spend their energy working instead of driving. This takes discipline, but self managed teams can go a long way towards correcting focal drift as peers hold one another accountable. The team rises or falls together, so they are direct in their feedback.

Leaders such as Virgin's Richard Branson have embraced the idea of open leave policies; take your vacations when you like, and don't worry about logging your sick days, just get your work done. This lets people avoid stressing about how many days they have to take or lose, and perhaps surprisingly many end up taking even less time off for vacations than they might otherwise. This policy lets them live a more flexible life, able to craft work hours around the normal tasks and errands that surround us and hence lowering employee stress. Of course, good communication and reliable results are expected in return.

---

[29] http://www.leanenterprisebook.com/

Performance Problems and Termination

Always an unpleasant subject, it is nonetheless vital to understand when and how to call it quits with an employee. While agile methods don't really address this subject directly, there are examples of companies trying to apply the principles with some success.

Cohesive teams work together effectively, and this means everyone. A single bad apple can be a real problem in a five or six person team. It helps if members can take action fairly directly to fix these problems themselves in the spirit of self management. Some teams at Capital One years ago tried a system wherein they literally voted people off the island. One that I observed used a ⅔ vote of confidence quarterly to determine if team members stayed or went. Note that this was generally a relocation elsewhere organizationally rather than a termination. What was interesting was that it rarely seemed to actually be employed to remove someone. The transparency of the environment led to poor performers often leaving of their own accord.

At The Motley Fool, problem employees are offered a generous severance package of a month's pay per year of employment up to a year, plus 30 days of COBRA and a placement program. 80% take it, but if not, they are paired with a coach to seek lateral opportunities in their role or within the company. The Fool feels that clear policies like these help managers take care of hard situations more readily, which in turn yields the tightly knit corporate ladder-free environment they desire. It lets managers spend their energy on top performers instead of struggling to improve those who won't help themselves. Toxic employees drain energy, and in a company with less than 400 people, excessive babysitting is an especially unappealing way to spend it.

Rigorous transparency can surface problems in a manner where they are easier to address and even take care of themselves on occasion. Self-managing teams are really peer-managed teams, so ensuring that people can be honest with one another about performance issues and have relatively painless channels for remedying them is important.

Summary - Working Together

Create a work environment wherein people can easily connect to one another while taking into account the needs of focus and privacy. Collocation is very important for complex interactions and making human connections, but virtual teams can be highly effective if properly prepared and equipped.

Agile feedback systems allow for the dynamic jobs that practitioners are expected to have, encouraging safe experimentation. They are quick and focused, and take into account the perspectives of team and organization as well as that of the individual.

Performance management in agile organizations is often a heavily peer-driven affair. When people must leave a job, make it easy for them to either find something else or to be relieved of their duties in a humane fashion that managers will not hesitate to utilize when needed.

Activities to Try

Hold a Daily Scrum with Your Team

Get your team started with one of the most popular and easy to implement agile patterns, the daily stand-up meeting. One nice way to run it is as follows:

1. Gather your team around your Story board (or some other visualization of your current work)
2. Ask the team what Stories have been finished since yesterday, and update their status. The transparency of this update helps eliminate other unnecessary status meetings by making it obvious what everyone is doing.

3. Ask what Stories are on deck for today. Look for opportunities for the team to collaborate around these jobs.
4. Ask if there are any blockers keeping work from getting completed. Don't brainstorm solutions yet, you'll do that just after the meeting.
5. Close the main meeting. At this point, "huddles" should spawn. These are mini-meetings that happen only between people who will be collaborating directly, hence avoiding wasting everyone else's time.

Keep in mind that this meeting is about driving collaboration over gathering status. It is meant to eliminate the need for other meetings by providing a quick and easy way to align people who are working toward a common goal and help them organize their work.

Hold an HR Retrospective

As people work within a given situation, they begin to understand it more, and can hence adapt their processes, tools and methods to better address it. Here's how to run a simple Scrum retrospective with your team and get the process started:

1. Have each person describe their state of mind in one word.
2. Review the purpose and agenda, adjusting as necessary.
3. Create a matrix with the quadrants "Happy," "Sad," "Idea" and "Appreciation."
4. The team silently generates thoughts on stickies populate this matrix, then places them in the appropriate quadrants.
5. Each person writes one improvement idea on an index card.
6. The team silently sorts the improvement ideas from highest to lowest impact.
7. Further sort into things the team can do alone, and things for which they require help.

8. Discuss the top few improvement ideas that are viable by the team and high impact, then the ones that will require additional stakeholders and potentially effort. Select one item from each category (you will do this again, don't get overambitious).

9. Each person raises between one and five fingers (a "fist of five") of five to indicate their support for actually implementing the top few improvement ideas.

10. Place the selected Improvement card on your Story Board.

11. Review the results at your next retrospective (every couple of weeks is a good cadence), and repeat.

12. Celebrate and share successes with other teams through lightweight field trips, brown bags and occasional unconferences.

Polyskill your HR Team

Here's a simple plan for introducing the idea of generalizing specialism into your HR team:

1. Start describing your jobs as team-level goals, rather than individual tasks. For instance, write "Revamp Performance Management System" rather than "Write Performance Management Interview Agenda - Jeremy."

2. Pick a handful of current jobs, and have a working session with your team to look for places where currently serialized processes can be made more concurrent, so that cycles like writing and editing, or designing and approving, can be done at the same time.

3. Encourage team members to pair up directly and learn about one another's skill sets while working. Activities like approvals can often be eliminated altogether this way, as reviews can happen in real time. You should start to notice fewer handoffs at this point.

4. Have a retrospective where the team discuss what they've learned from one another. Have them offer up skills that they hold which they would like to share with others, and then hold a skills marketplace to connect mentors and mentees where there is shared interest.

5. Try to find opportunities for these pairs to work together in your next set of jobs.

You'll find your teams working more closely together in no time, and then you can show other departments how to do it!

Chapter 7 — Learning & Professional Development

Since agility infers the steady adoption of new skills and appearance of new situations, a strong training and career development system is a necessity, both to prepare teams initially and provide a mechanism for growth and adaptation in the face of change.

Agile Career Planning

There is more than one way in which agile career paths may be carved, and that is at the heart of their appeal. HR policies should create a growth-oriented environment, encouraging and supporting career paths that meander, expand and contract with guidance but not undue constraint. This makes employees more versatile and keeps them challenged.

A core tenet of agile teams is the notion of generalizing specialism or versatility, the idea that people are typically capable of more than their job titles imply and that skill sets should expand and overlap in a complementary fashion. Simple examples are a developer that also assists in testing or a recruiter that contributes to visual design. In small teams this is especially critical, as the more that work can be jointly understood and executed, the less likely it is that bottlenecks will occur while waiting for a single expert to become available. Team members who understand the whole of a job and one another's contributions also excel at holistically great design, while siloed activities tend to hurt both speed and innovation.

This notion of learning laterally about the skills of one's peers implies an inherent flexibility of role. So, a Scrum Master in many organizations might formally be a Senior Developer, or a Chief Product Owner a Program Manager. While one might hire an individual to act as a coach or Product Owner, it is common to see him shift to other duties over time, aligning the labels more closely with roles than job titles.

While having specific desired qualities clearly defined for agile positions in an organization still seems the exception rather than the rule, the common factors tend to include, in order of importance:

- Agile experience - People who have seen agile in different environments will much better understand how to flex teams without breaking them, and experienced team members will be better at working constructively together in such dynamic environments.
- Agile education, both receiving and giving - A common way to assess this is something akin to a teaching hospital, where the mantra is "see one, do one, teach one." A nascent Scrum Master might first acquire training, observe coaches and teams in action and do some self learning (see one), apprentice with a veteran Scrum Master and pick up more responsibilities over time under their tutelage, eventually leading their own team (do one), and finally tutor other fresh Scrum Masters and lead training sessions of their own to prove true mastery (teach one).
- Breadth of authority - This primarily applies to leadership positions such as Chief Scrum Masters and Chief Product Owners. Those who lead very important or large scale initiatives, manage larger budgets and take bigger risks on behalf of an organization will tend to earn greater salaries.
- Organizational seniority - This can be attached to both duration and position; so, a 5-year veteran would get more than a 3-year one, and a Director more than a Manager.

These factors might even be linked to pay levels, sometimes in a very structured fashion (e.g. Product Owner Level 3 with 12 points of additional Skills = $165,000), and sometimes more subjectively. Specific desirable skills, such as familiarity with certain toolsets, languages, domains and so forth, are provided as personal building blocks for practitioners to acquire over time, thus increasing their value and raising their salary. Companies have even "gamified" this growth by presenting the skills in a bingo-like template that can be filled in over time.

The core of agile career path design is providing access to new skills in a way that the organizationally transparently and tangibly values, so that new workers are encouraged to deepen and broaden their skill sets over time. Then you make it easy for them to acquire the information they need to grow.

Supporting Continuous Learning

If someone is to grow continuously they must be able to acquire knowledge when and how they will. This means supplying education through multiple channels and formats. Libraries of short instructional videos, podcasts, articles, interactive learning applications, communities of interest and brief virtual instructor led training options are but a few examples of this versatile, learner-driven stance.

HR practitioners should build learning curriculums which make development paths clear and tie knowledge acquisition to career progression. Nationwide Insurance's Tree of Knowledge is one example that combines training on core agile techniques for every-one with role-specific courses for developers, testers, requirements analysts and iteration managers (Scrum Masters). Moving up the Tree is tied to progression in the company.

It is important that learning be validated. Many organizations adopt something akin to the *learning hospital* model, which is *see one, do one, teach one*. After being trained on a new skill, one must both demonstrate direct proficiency and teach someone else about the skill before designated as adept. Intelligent surveys have also begun to emerge which can paint a clear picture of competence and confidence over time, bringing solid data to the party.

Agile Training & Certification Programs

While agile training programs abound these days, the most prominent certifying bodies are the Scrum Alliance, Scrum.org, ICAgile and Scaled Agile, Inc. The Scrum Alliance offers Certified Scrum Master (CSM), Certified Product Owner (CSPO) and Certified Scrum Developer (CSD) training among others, and is currently the provider with the broadest reach. Scrum.org offers similar content under the Professional Scrum Master designation. ICAgile offers a broad range of courses for all agile disciplines, including testers and leaders, as well as some of the first offerings specifically tailored towards business agility. The Scaled Agile Institute offers a host of classes designed around their proprietary Scaled Agile Framework® which cover topics ranging all the way from the team to the enterprise.

At the organizational level, industry certifications are meant to grow skills and knowledge from a source of authority, and develop a shared understanding and vocabulary. Finding an appropriate certification program depends largely on what agile methods may have already been adopted and the level of consulting and scaling support that your company needs from the industry. This would be a discussion to have with your stakeholders in other departments.

Certifications can also function as motivators for individuals by enhancing their career credentials, and perhaps by garnering rewards in the form of recognition, compensation or authority. Explore them and see what makes the most sense for your organization.

Agile Coaching

The problem with training alone is that it tends to be both time-bound and generic. When people hit real-world problems, direct guidance from a master can avoid lost momentum and frustration. Scrum Masters should be able to coach people, but the term *agile coach* often implies a higher level of expertise, acting across the organization while Scrum Masters focus on teams.

Many companies hire external coaches to get things started with an external mandate and deeper expertise. This can be a highly impactful strategy, but make sure that you have apprentices ready to learn from those experts and pick up the reigns themselves or a codependent situation could develop that slows growth of internal capability.

Innovation and Marketing Events

As arbiters of corporate culture, HR professionals must understand how to spread the word about agility and why it matters. While standard corporate communication channels still apply, there are some interesting new approaches worth exploring.

Make results public, whether positive or not. A key idea in agile circles is that failure can be a learning opportunity. Showing where things have been tried, foundered and then adapted to succeed can convey this mindset so that people feel safe to experiment. Publicity yields both accountability and celebration.

One very popular way to host information-sharing, community-building agile events is the open space or unconference. Open space events have no preordained program; participants suggest their own topics and sign up to attend in real time. Sessions like this have always been popular among practitioners at the large agile conferences, because they allow for deeper, more interactive conversations based upon the interests of the moment. Topics build on one another and sprout from chance inspiration over the course of the event.

A side benefit in an organizational context is the onus on attendees to bring good stories and teach one another, dramatically superior to having some central committee plan it all out and then just hope people will engage. Unconferences[30] are one way to facilitate an open space session, with BarCamp[31] a popular example that started as a technical event but has since been adopted to all manner of topics.

Hack days such as Atlassian's ShipIt Day[32] are also a popular theme. These offer participants a chance to enjoy some autonomy by choosing what they'd like to build, how and with whom. They typically have a loosely structured format, but almost always conclude with a public demo of some sort. Results of these sessions might end up being used as prototypes for new projects, they might be useful as tweaks or fixes to existing products and services, or they might be used simply for learning and entertainment purposes. The benefit of such sessions is engagement via autonomy; everyone enjoys the freedom to act as they choose at times, especially when there is an opportunity for recognition.

Summary - Learning and Professional Development

HR professionals must create agile career paths that are purposefully dynamic, with many opportunities for learning on one's own and with others. There are myriad well regarded training and certification programs available at this point.

Agile coaching can help kickstart teams, getting them over common hurdles that can be overwhelming to the uninitiated. These are often external initially, but should be quickly grown from within.

Events such as innovation days can provide highly public forums for promoting both the personal and business benefits of agile approaches. They often follow formats which are explicitly based on agile life cycles. While no substitute for ongoing innovation programs, they can be a good way to generate fun and excitement.

---

[30] http://unconference.net/unconferencing-how-to-prepare-to-attend-an-unconference/

[31] https://en.wikipedia.org/wiki/BarCamp

[32] https://www.atlassian.com/company/shipit

Activities to Try

Get Educated in Lean and Agile

Not a very radical suggestion, but a sensible and easy one! Discover a role for which you feel an affinity. Perhaps you like coaching people and tuning processes for maximum efficiency with minimal pain: a Scrum Master class would make sense. If you prefer creative design, presentation and marketing, a Product Owner class could be more appropriate. Or maybe you're into systems thinking and holistic organizational design, in which case a Certified Agile Leadership or scaling class might suit you best.

These courses tend to be about two days long and between one and two thousand dollars, a small price to pay for understanding the sea change you're going to experience. If that's too deep an investment, there are plenty of freely available learning resources in the form of articles, videos and more. Check out the Reading List at the end of the book for some suggestions.

Create a Colleague Letter of Understanding (CLOU)

A tool used by the tomato processing company Morning Star to drive self management, the CLOU is meant to outline the dependencies between people, so that they can manage their joint activities smoothly together. It works alongside an "advisement process," whereby people can make decisions on their own, they simply must tell others about them first.

You can create a CLOU alone or in concert with a mentor or peer, but it should certainly be reviewed by anyone involved to ensure accuracy and alignment. One way is as follows:

1. Note your current Short Term (1-3 months) and Long Term Development Goals.
2. Note your current major Responsibilities (the top 6-10, not too many) in one column.

3. In the next column, note your current Activities for each Responsibility, and your Authority Level in each (e.g. Responsible, Approval, Supportive).
4. In the same column, note the key Colleagues with whom you interact for each Activity.
5. Pick a few Activities that you feel need some attention, and which align well with your current Goals. A mix of short-term and long-term attention is nice.
6. In the third and final column, note a Target Result that you might reasonably hope to hit within the next month for these Activities, and a handful of specific Stepping Stones to get you there.

That's it; meet next month, review and update with your mentor, and you've got one of the basic tools of self management at your command.

Host an HR Games Day

Get your team into the spirit of fun-filled sharing with a collaborative learning event where games and exercises are exchanged.

1. Ask team members to think of some games or interactive activities that they have either tried in a professional context, or simply feel might have implications for learning. Give them at least a month to prepare.
2. Create an open space board that has time slots for each session (see below) with space for at least two sticky notes or index cards each
3. Have participants bring up and quickly describe their ideas as they place them on this board during Scheduling.
4. The overall agenda might look like this:

- 9:00 - 9:30 Continental Breakfast
- 9:30 - 9:40 Opening

- 9:40 - 10:00 Opening Circle and Scheduling - Describe games here
- 10:00 - 10:45 Session 1
- 10:45 - 11:00 Break
- 11:00 - 11:45 Session 2
- 11:45-12:45 Lunch
- 12:45-1:00 Propose New Sessions
- 1:00 - 1:45 Session 3
- 1:45 - 2:00 Break
- 2:00 - 2:45 Session 4
- 2:45 - 3:00 Break
- 3:00 - 3:45 Session 5
- 3:45 - 4:00 Break
- 4:00 - 5:00 Closing Reception

Events like this can be thrilling, educational and great team building experiences all at once.

Conclusion

Now is the time to start experimenting with agility in HR. As leaders and builders of people, you have the best chance of making our organizations into the invigorating, lithe, creative powerhouses they must be to survive and thrive in days to come. This idea of agility in HR is a relatively new one, so your intrepid explorations may well break new ground and provide fresh inspiration for future generations.

Once you understand the tenets of agility yourself, you can effectively support your company and its people as they adopt and expand the usage of these methods themselves. Nearly every aspect of organizations has the potential to be affected by the rigorous demands of agile methods, and it is your job to ensure that change is in positive direction.

We have included a host of *Activities to Try* at the end of each section. Pick a few that sound like they would make a difference and get started. There are plenty of self-led learning opportunities, training classes, books and coaches out there on the topics of lean and agile as well. Find an option that meets your needs and get familiar with the principles. It will not be too painful, as these methods were designed by humans for humans.

Good luck, and go change the world!

Reading List

- Whats Deming Got to Do With Agile Software Development and Kanban by Dennis Stevens[33]
- Traditional HR has failed us! How to convince them to go Agile by Fabiola Eyholzer[34]
- Self-Selecting Teams by Amber King[35]
- Performance Discussions: Save the Scary for Halloween by Tracy Saunders[36]
- How HR Can Become Agile (and Why it Needs To) by Jeff Gothelf[37]
- The Machine That Changed the World, Lean Thinking, Womack & Jones
- Appreciative Inquiry[38]
- IDEO Design Thinking[39]
- Deloitte Global Human Capital Trends[40]
- Fast Company - Jared Lindzon, Welcome to the New Era of Human Resources[41]
- Scaled Agile Framework - Value Streams[42]

---

[33] https://blog.deming.org/2013/07/whats-deming-got-to-do-with-agile-software-development-and-kanban

[34] http://www.slideshare.net/FabiolaEyholzer/adventures-with-agile-traditional-hr-has-failed-us-how-to-convince-them-to-go-agile

[35] https://www.linkedin.com/pulse/self-selecting-teams-could-work-you-amber-king?trk=prof-post

[36] https://www.linkedin.com/pulse/performance-discussions-save-scary-halloween-tracy-saunders-pcc

[37] https://hbr.org/2017/06/how-hr-can-become-agile-and-why-it-needs-to

[38] https://appreciativeinquiry.case.edu/intro/whatisai.cfm

[39] http://www.ideou.com/pages/design-thinking

[40] https://www2.deloitte.com/content/dam/Deloitte/global/Documents/About-Deloitte/central-europe/ce-global-human-capital-trends.pdf

[41] https://www.fastcompany.com/3045829/the-new-rules-of-work/welcome-to-thenew-era-of-human-resources

[42] http://www.scaledagileframework.com/value-streams/

- LitheSpeed - No Projects[43]
- Scrum at Scale[44]
- Harvard Business Review - Ram Charan, Dominic Barton, Dennis Carey, People Before Strategy: A New Role for the CHRO[45]
- InfoQ - How Swarming Helps Agile Teams to Deliver[46]
- Mob Programming[47]
- Les McKeown - Predictable Success[48]
- Mike Cohn on the Scrum Master[49]
- Mike Cohn "Leader of the Band: Six Qualities of the Good Scrum Master"[50]
- Simon Sinek on Why Good Leaders Make You Feel Safe[51]
- John Shook - The Remarkable Chief Engineer[52]
- Agile Manifesto[53]
- Agile Leadership Academy[54]
- Declaration of Interdependence[55]
- Daniel Goleman - Focus: The Hidden Driver of Excellence[56]
- Fast Company - Chris Dannen, Inside GitHub's Super-Lean Management Strategy–And How It Drives Innovation[57]

---

[43] https://lithespeed.com/noprojects-need-projects/

[44] https://www.scrumatscale.com/scrum-at-scale-guide/

[45] https://hbr.org/2015/07/people-before-strategy-a-new-role-for-the-chro

[46] https://www.infoq.com/news/2013/02/swarming-agile-teams-deliver

[47] http://mobprogramming.org

[48] www.predictablesuccess.com

[49] https://www.mountaingoatsoftware.com/agile/scrum/scrummaster

[50] http://www.mountaingoatsoftware.com/articles/leader-of-the-band

[51] https://www.ted.com/talks/simon_sinek_why_good_leaders_make_you_feel_safe/transcript?language=en

[52] http://www.lean.org/shook/DisplayObject.cfm?o=906

[53] http://agilemanifesto.org

[54] http://www.agileleadershipacademy.com

[55] http://pmdoi.org

[56] https://www.amazon.com/Focus-Hidden-Excellence-Daniel-Golemanebook/dp/B00BATG220

[57] https://www.fastcompany.com/3020181/open-company/inside-githubs-super-leanmanagement-strategy-and-how-it-drives-innovation

- Dan Pink - Drive[58]
- Dan Ariely - What Makes us Feel Good About our Work?[59]
- Lazlo Bock - Work Rules[60]
- Obie Fernandez and Trevor Owens - The Lean Enterprise[61]
- Unconference[62]
- BarCamp[63]
- Atlassian Ship-It[64]

---

[58] http://www.danpink.com/books/drive/
[59] https://www.ted.com/talks/dan_ariely_what_makes_us_feel_good_about_our_work
[60] www.workrules.net
[61] http://www.leanenterprisebook.com/
[62] http://unconference.net/unconferencing-how-to-prepare-to-attend-anunconference/
[63] https://en.wikipedia.org/wiki/BarCamp
[64] https://www.atlassian.com/company/shipit

About the Author

Arlen Bankston is one of the two founders and owners of LitheSpeed and cofounder of the Agile Leadership Academy. He has been actively involved in the application and evolution of Agile software development processes such as Scrum, Kanban and Extreme Programming for over a decade and a half. He is also a Lean Six Sigma Master Black Belt, and was an early adopter in the application of broader lean principles to agile methods to deepen theoretical understanding and drive organizational change. He was one of the earliest Certified ScrumMaster Trainers, and specializes in the role of the Product Owner, given an early career in product design and management. There, he leveraged principles of information architecture, interaction design and usability to develop innovative products that met customersâ€™ expressed and unspoken needs.

Arlen has led Agile and Lean deployment and managed process improvement projects at hundreds of clients in highly diverse industries, such as Marriott, Capital One, Neustar, CCP Games, T. Rowe Price, Freddie Mac, and the Armed Forces Benefits Association. His agile career began when he started exploring and speaking about the integration of interaction design and usability practices into Agile methodologies, and he is a regular speaker, trainer and organizer of at conferences around the world. He loves the depth, broad applicability and never-ending evolution of these methods, and it has kept him passionate about it all of these years.

Made in the
USA
Monee, IL